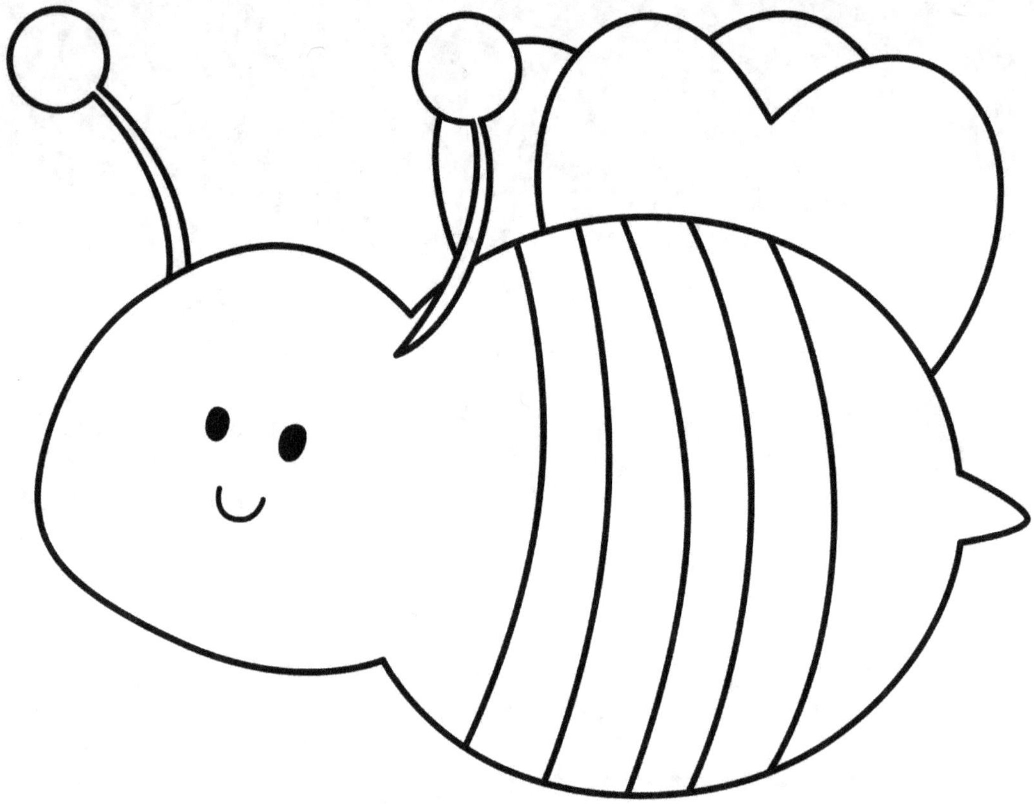

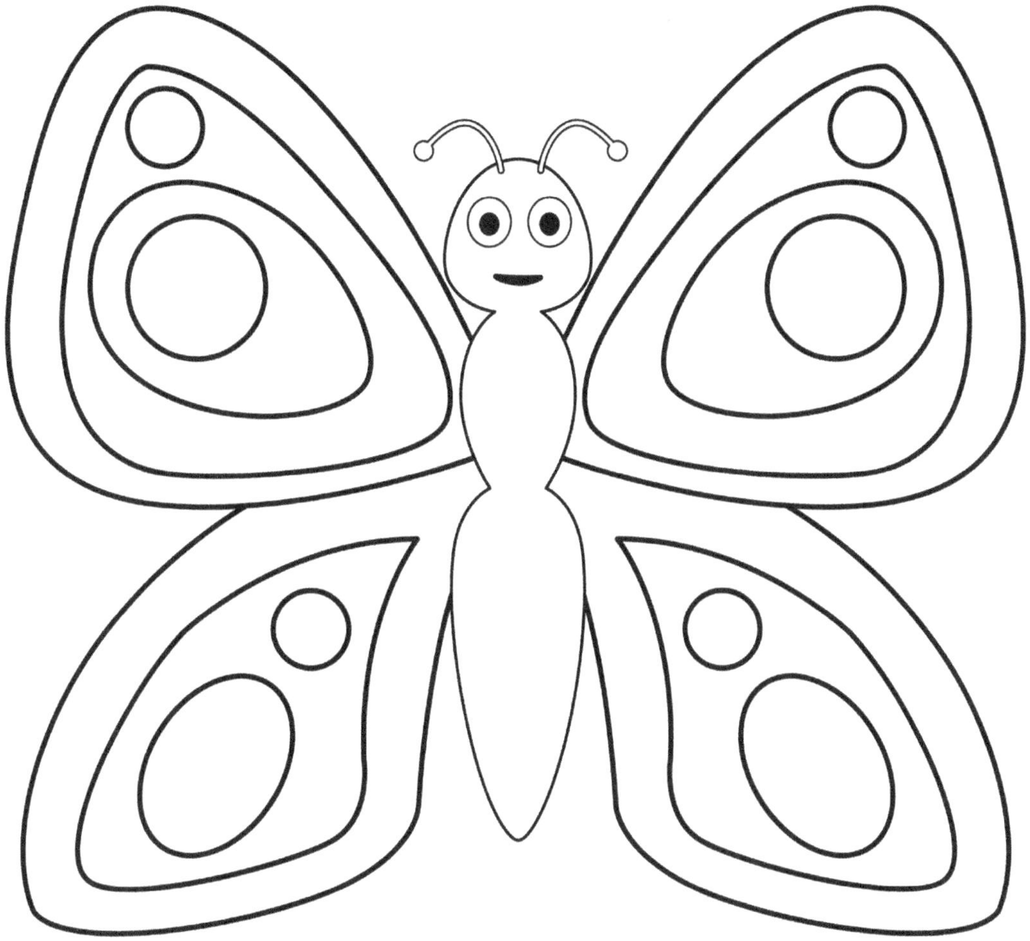

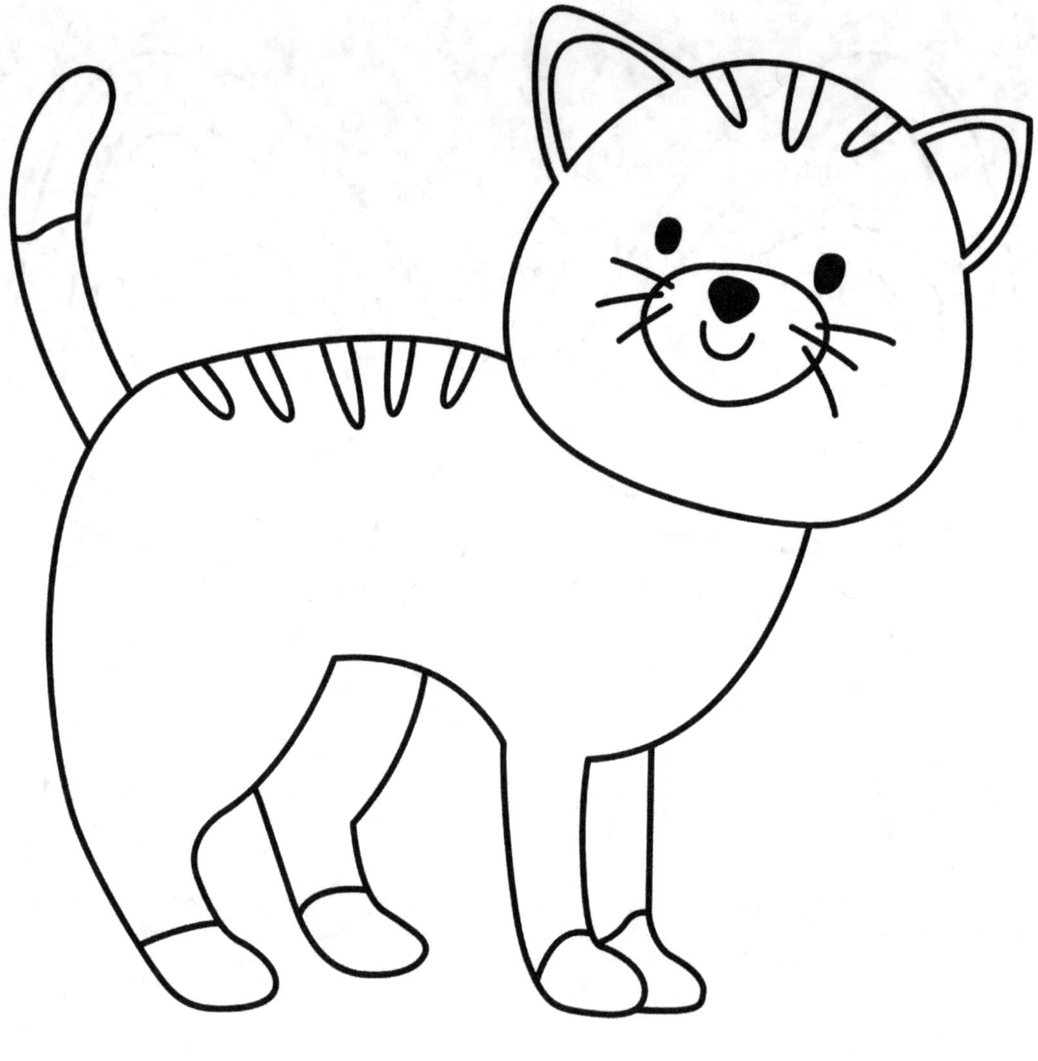

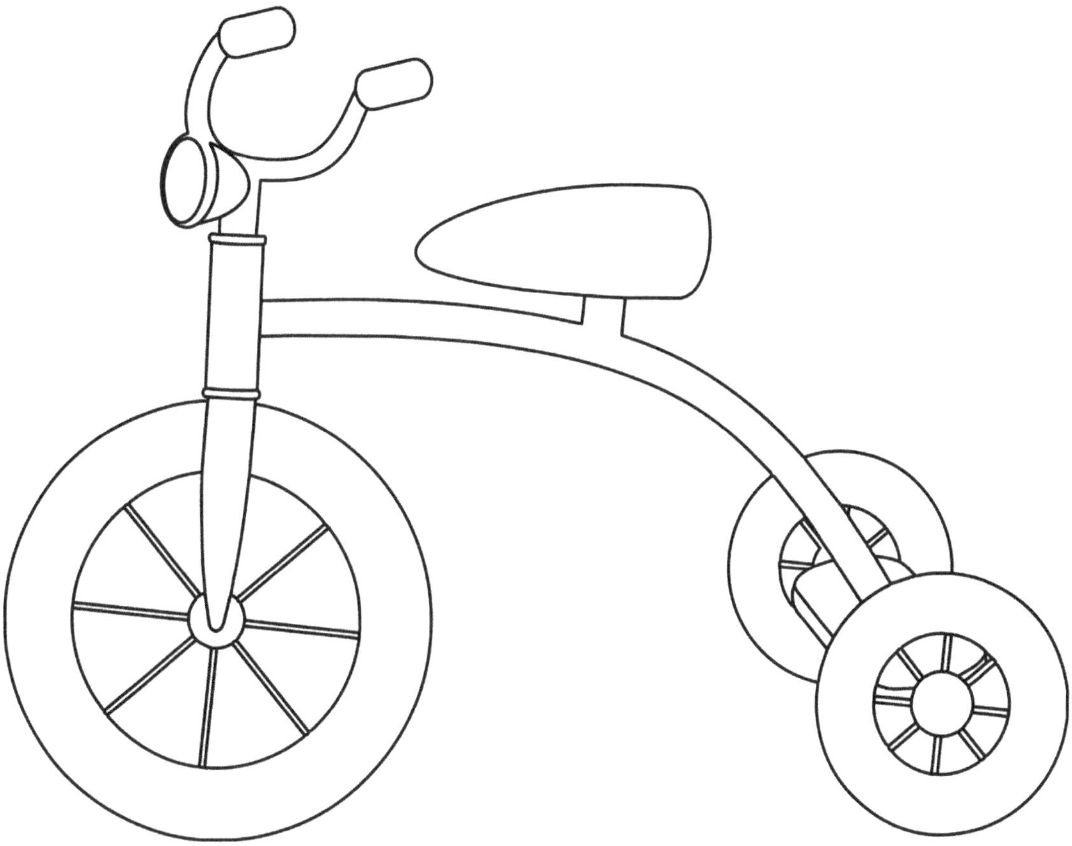

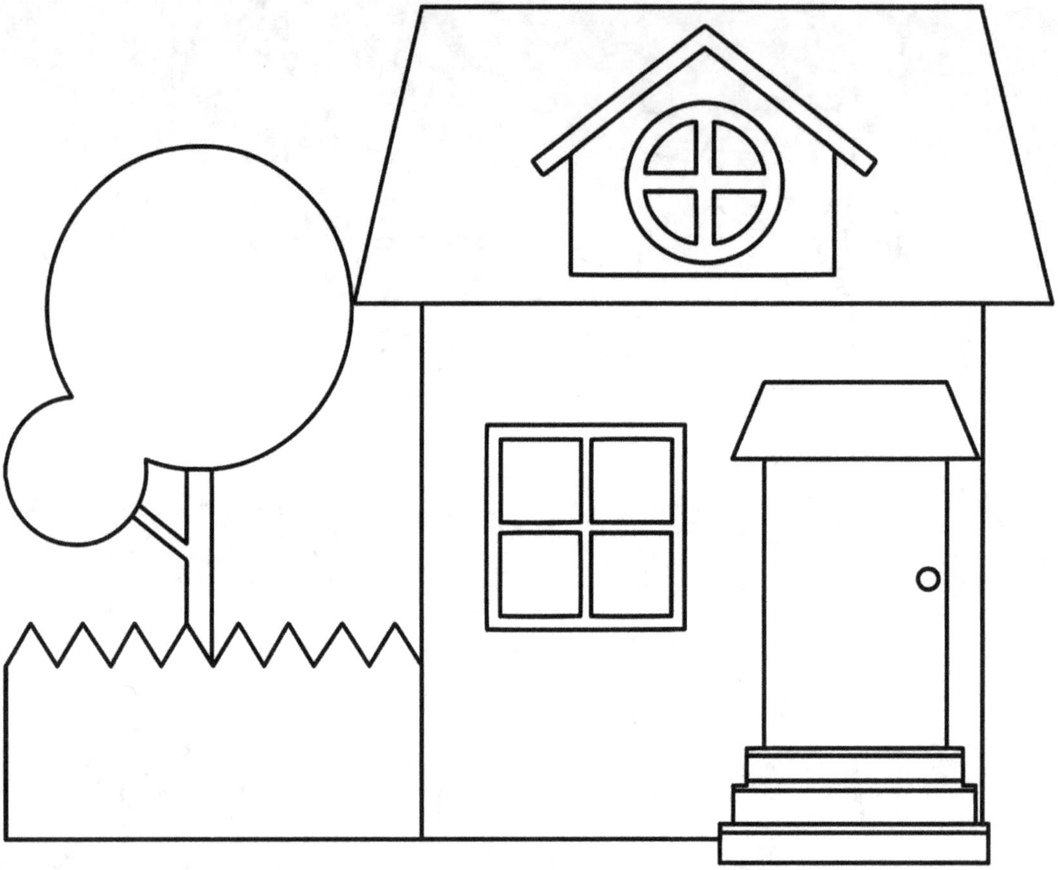

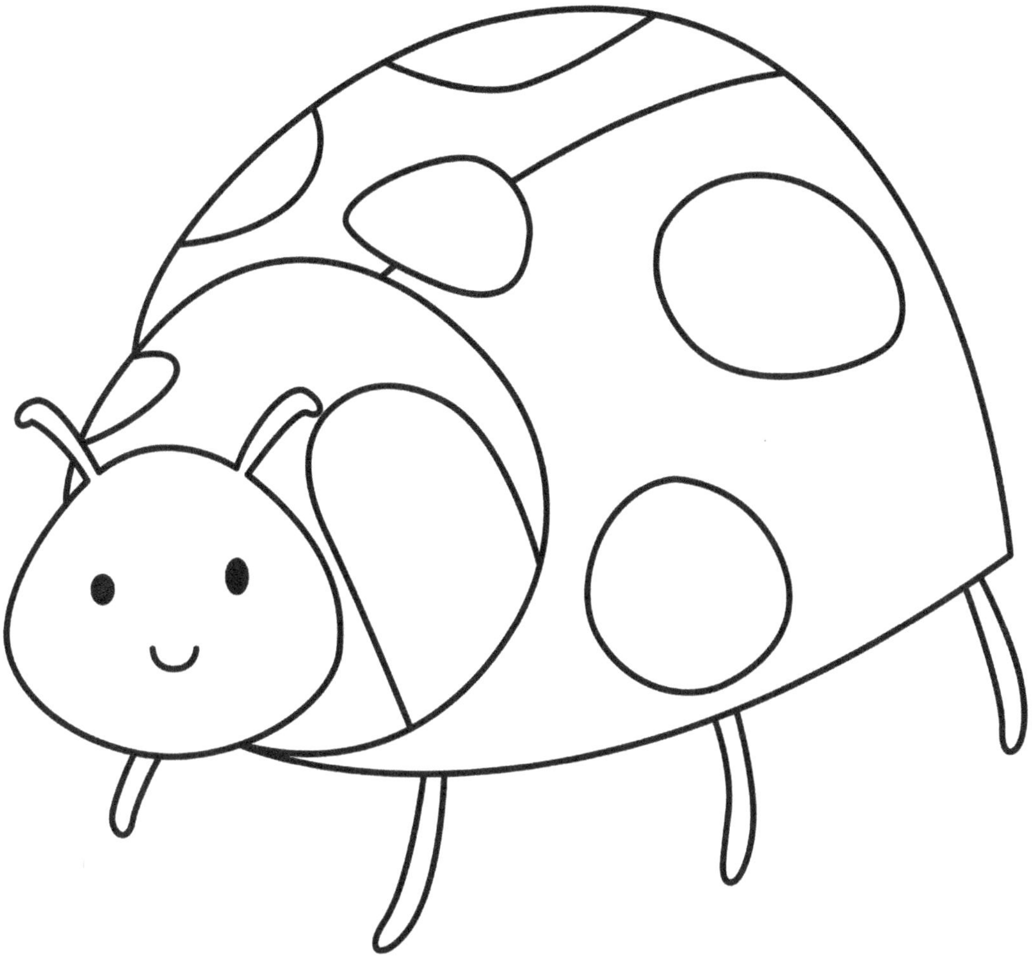

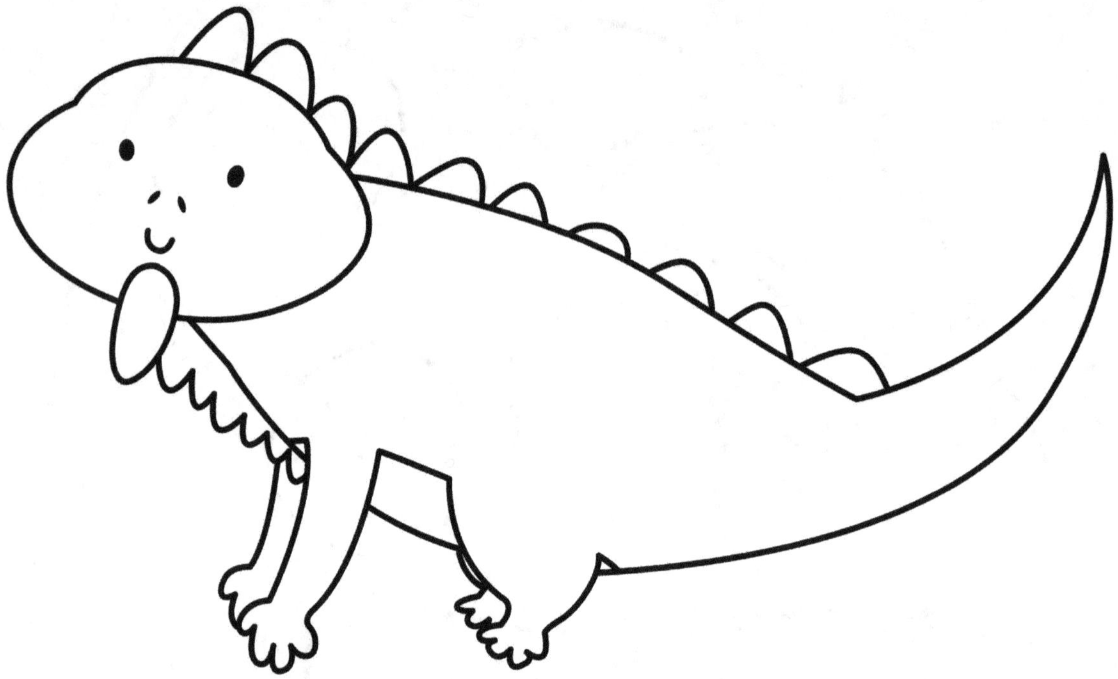

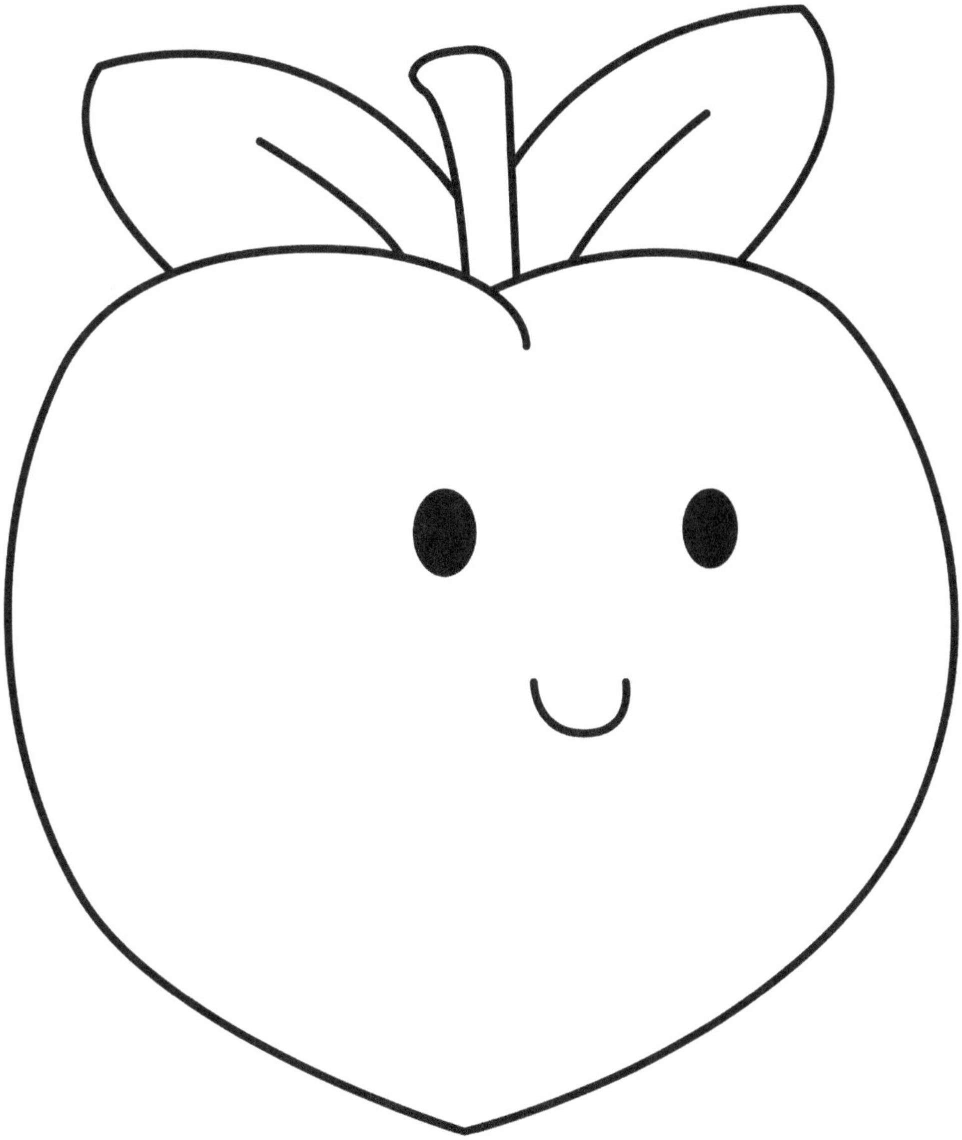

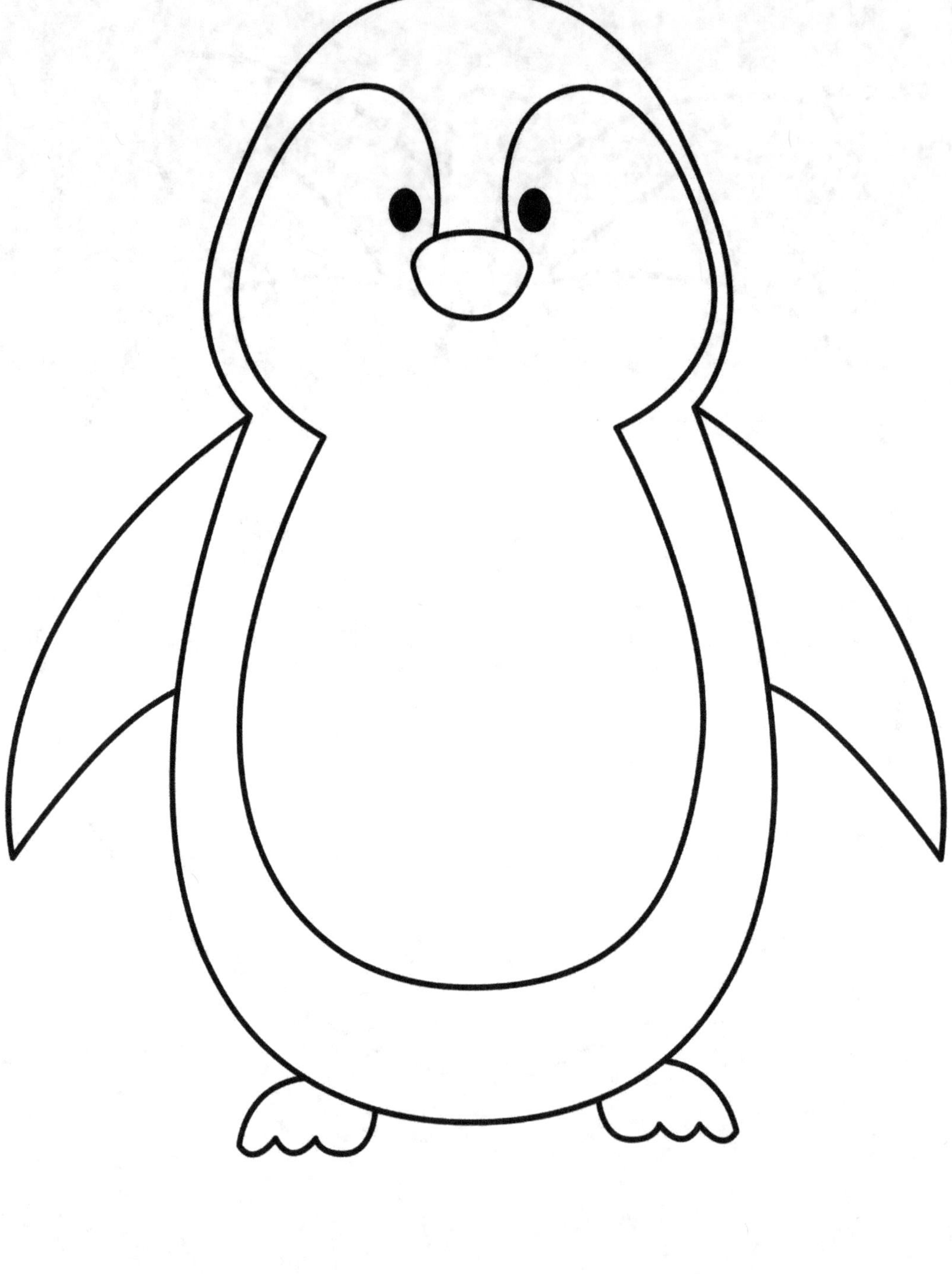

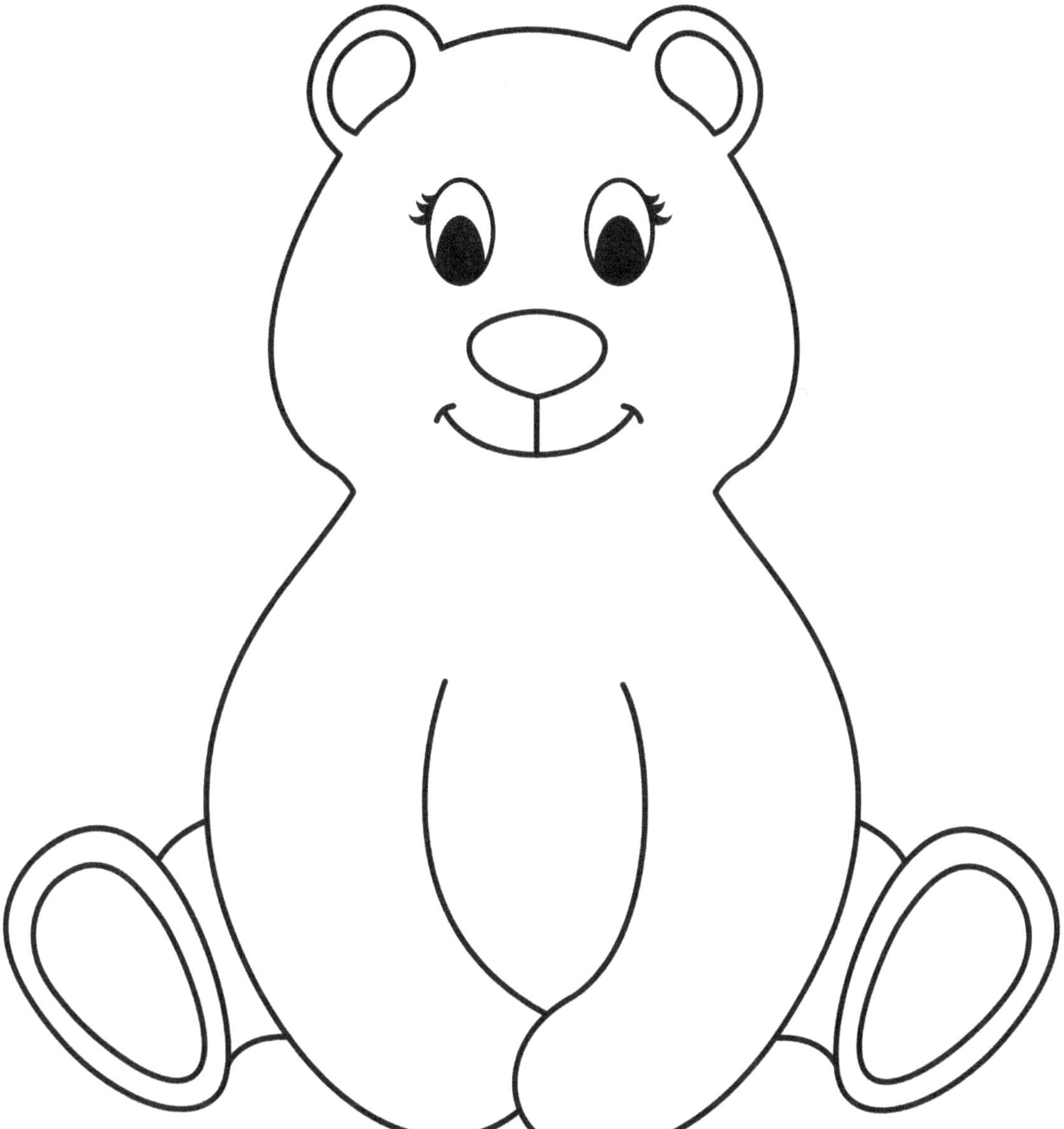

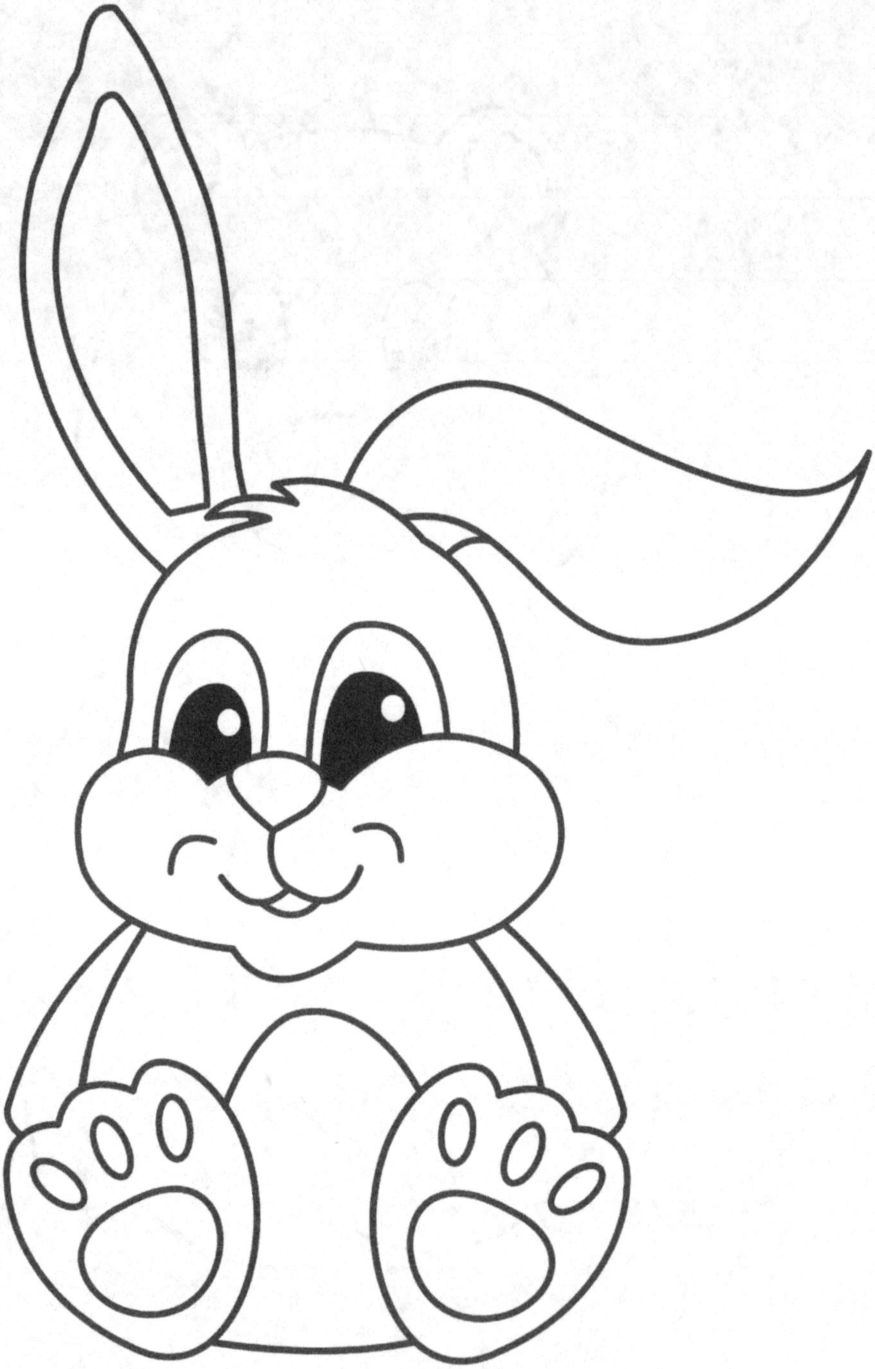

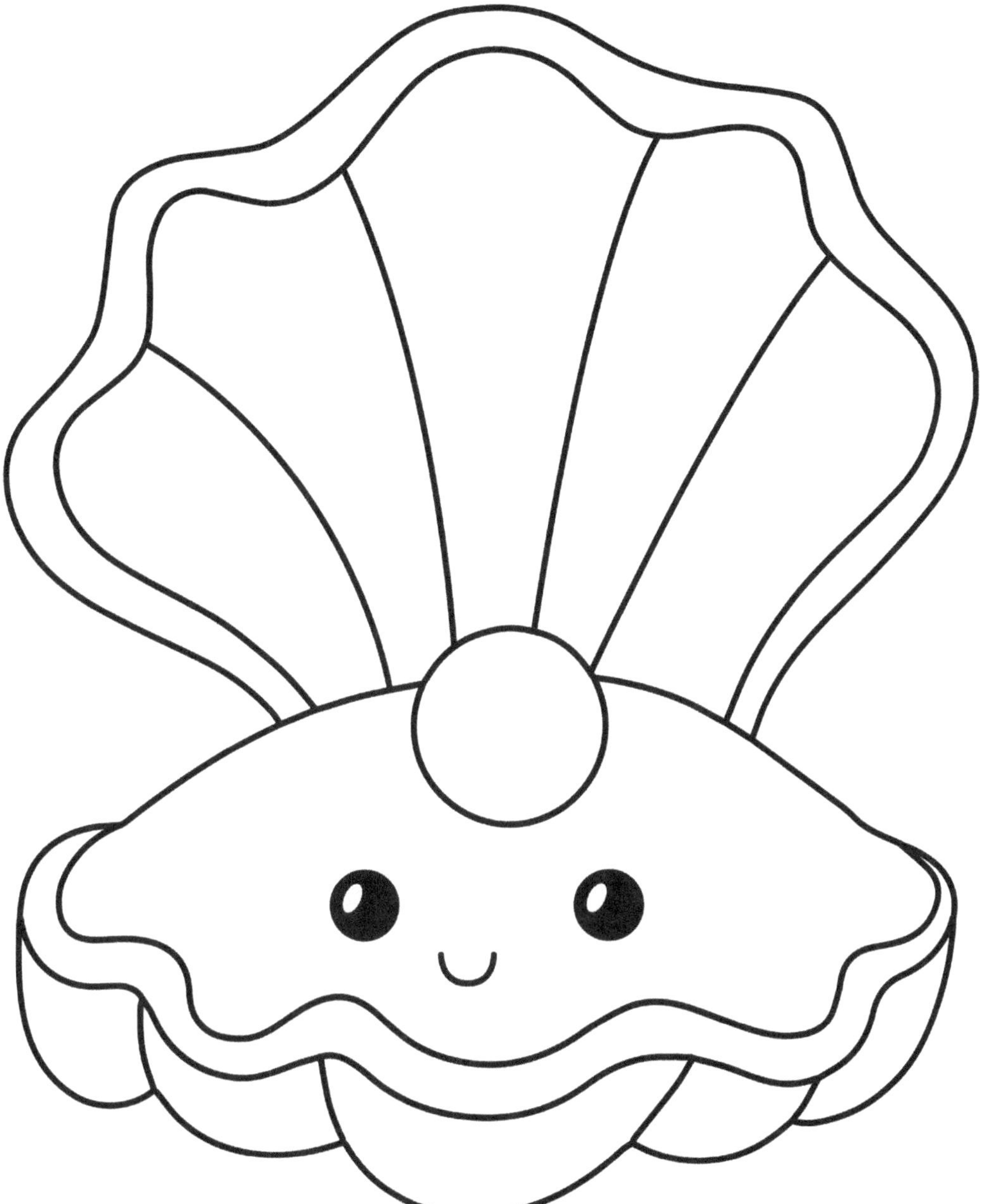

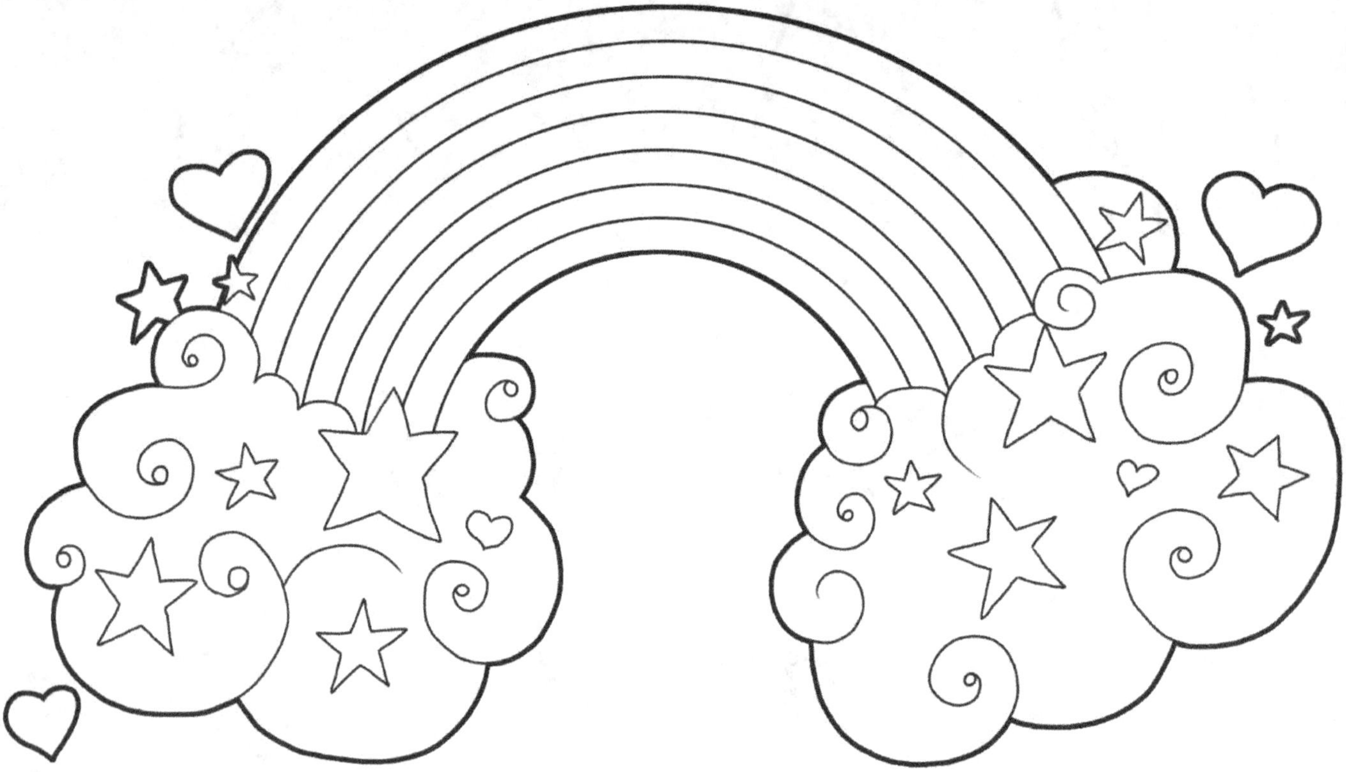

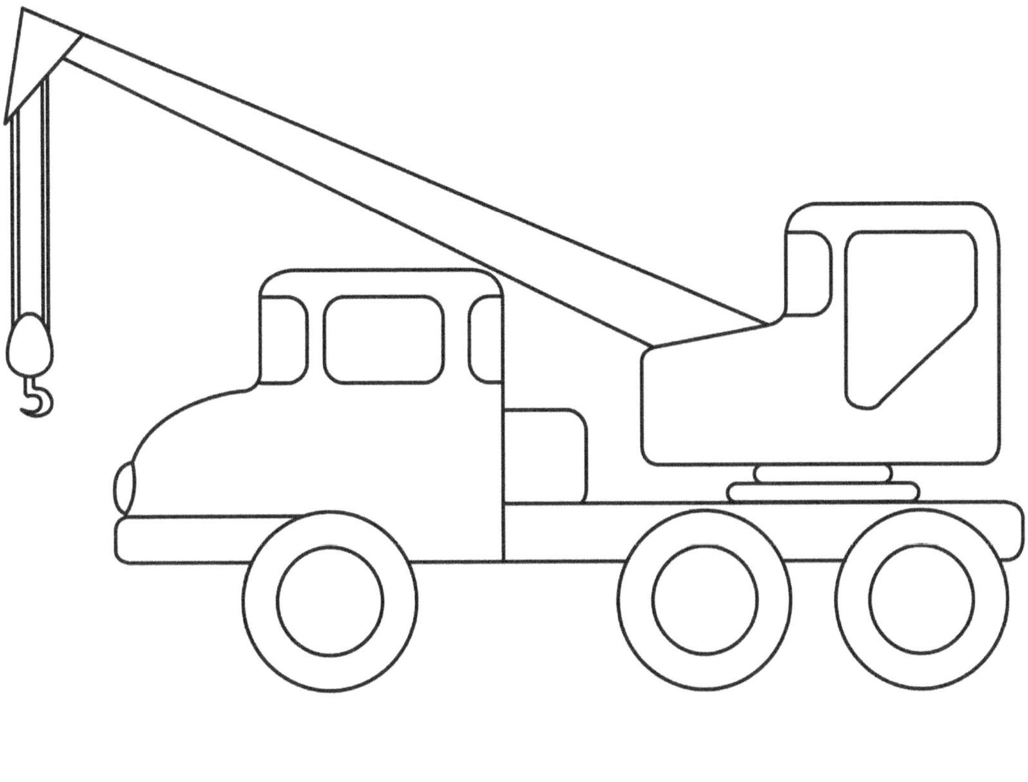

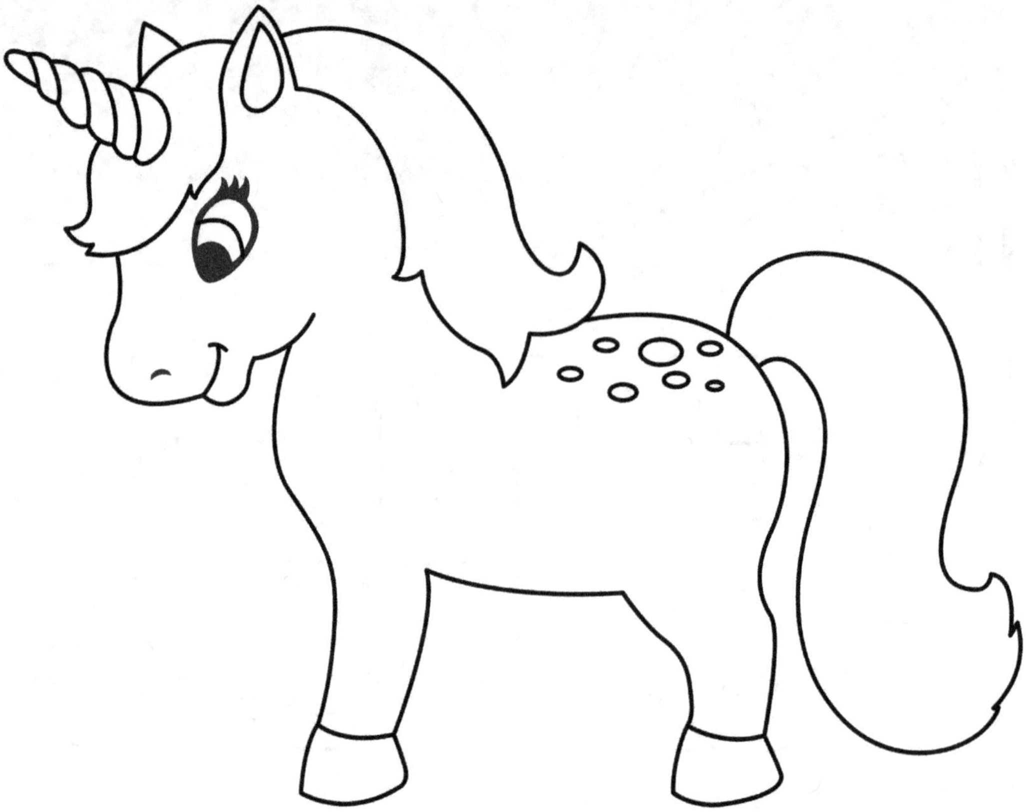

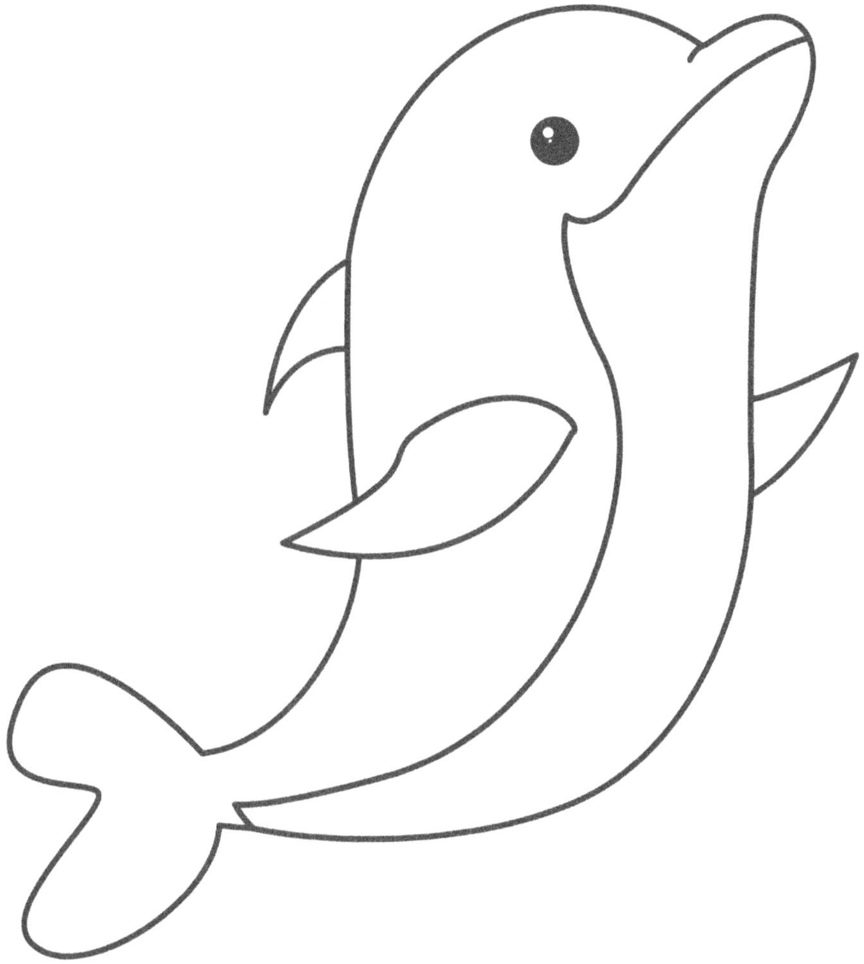

BONUS

holiday pages

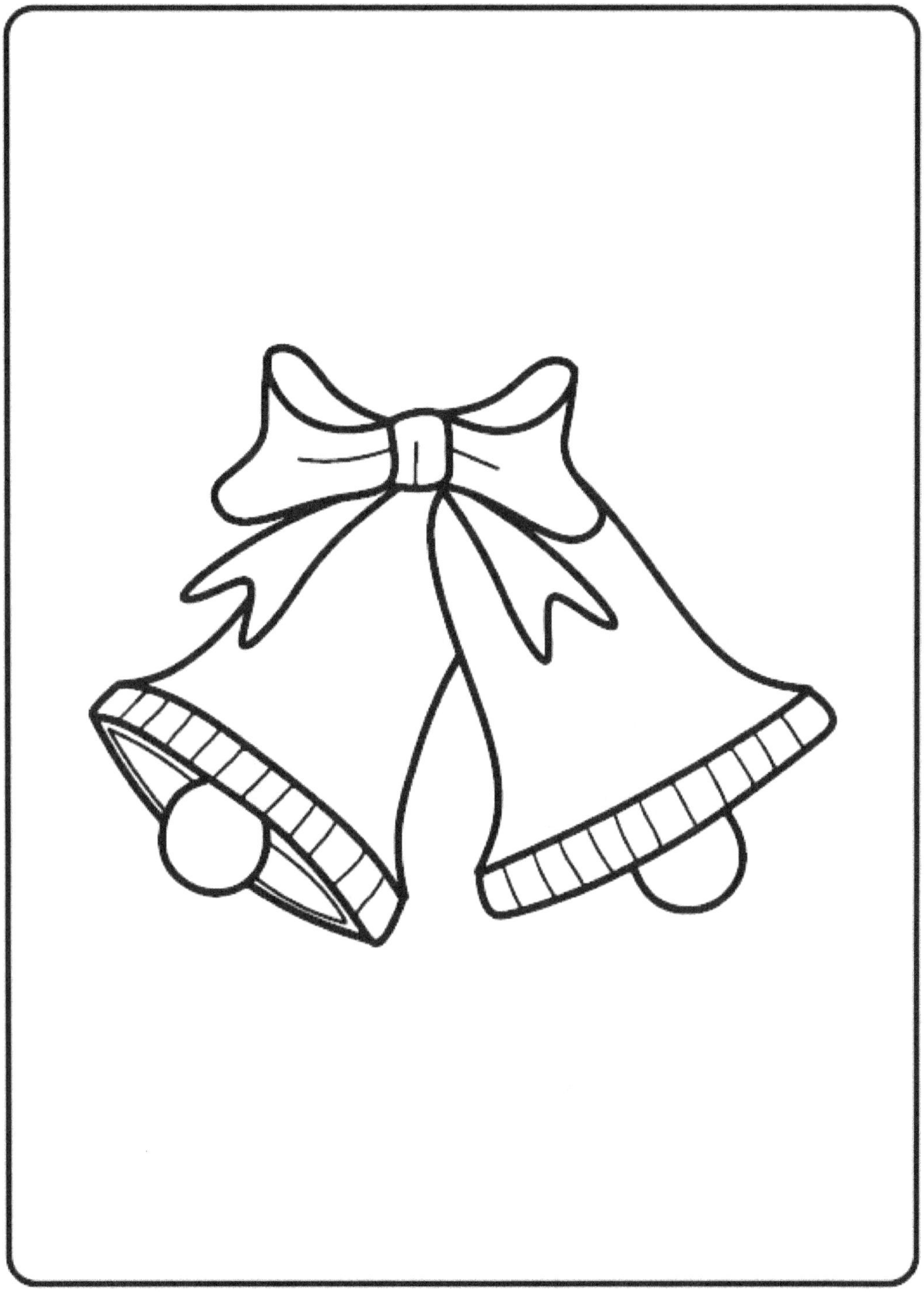

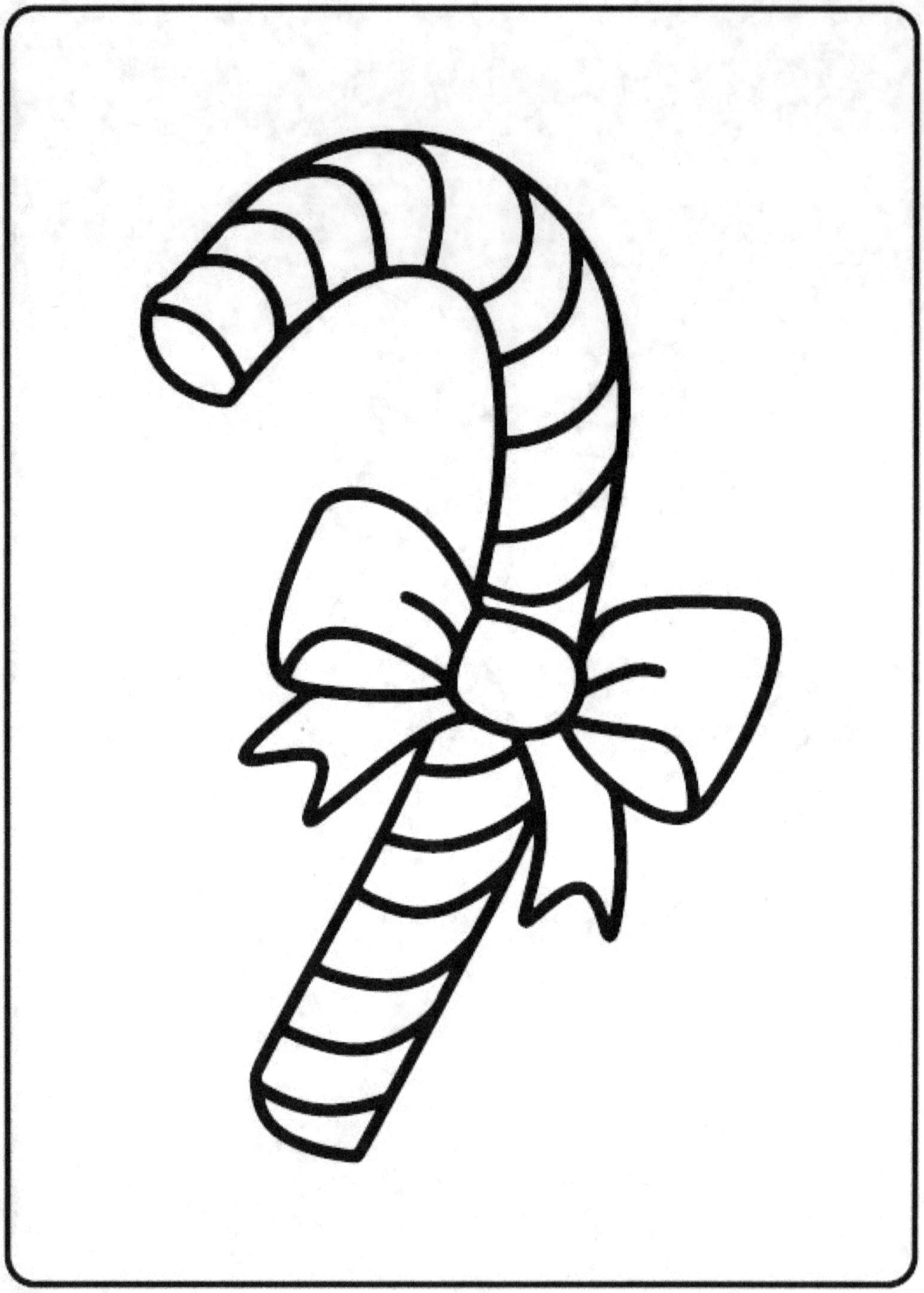

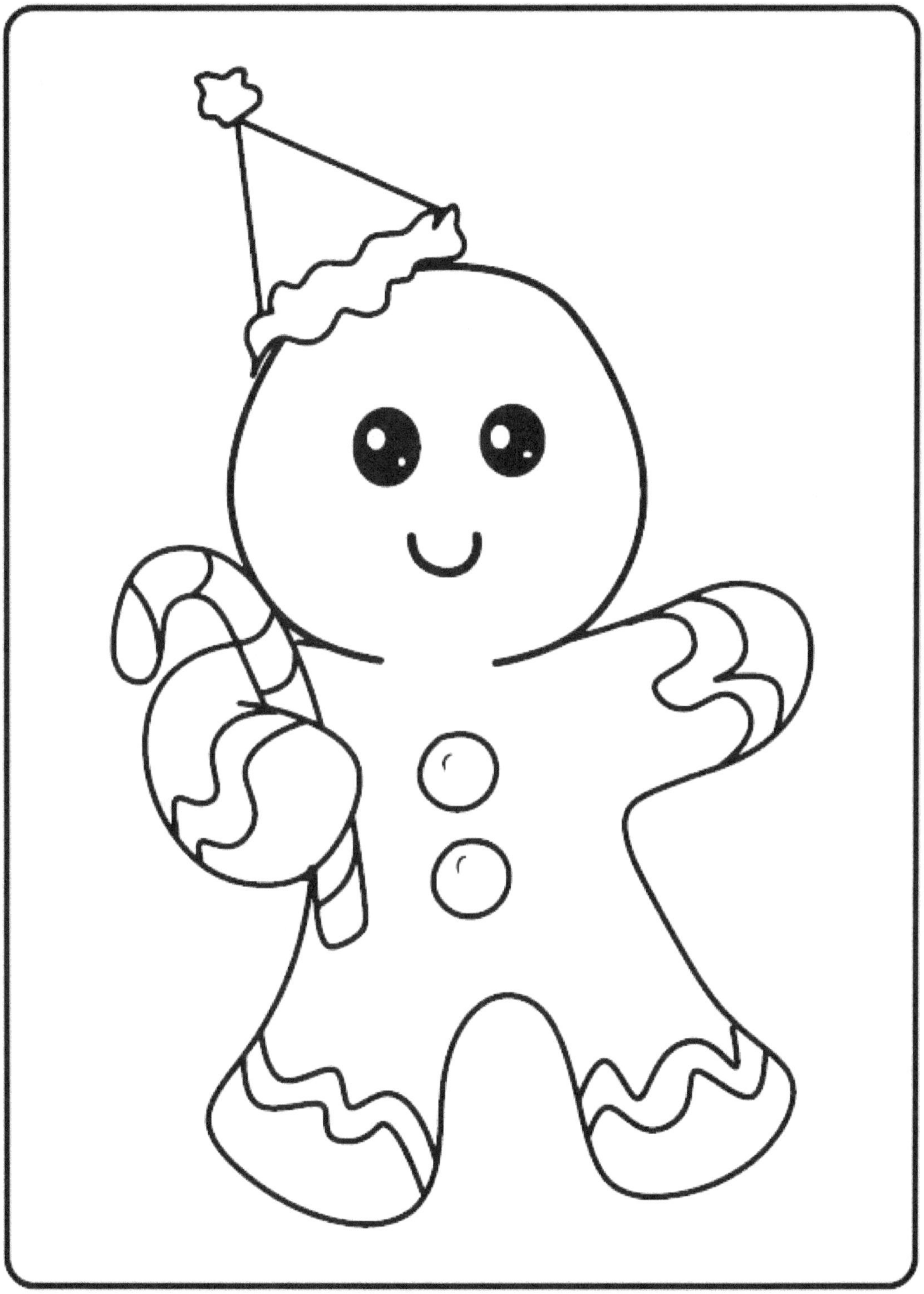

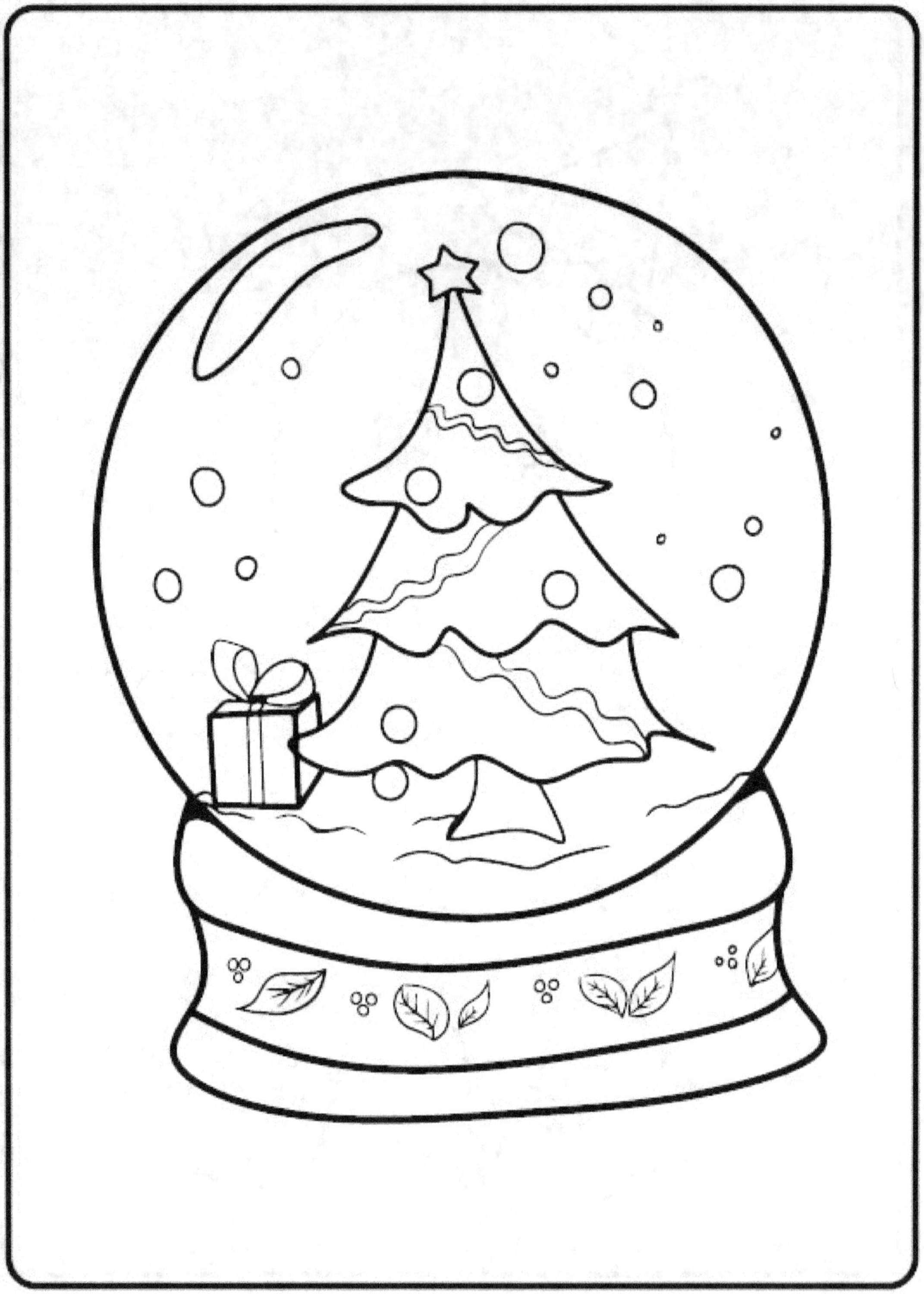

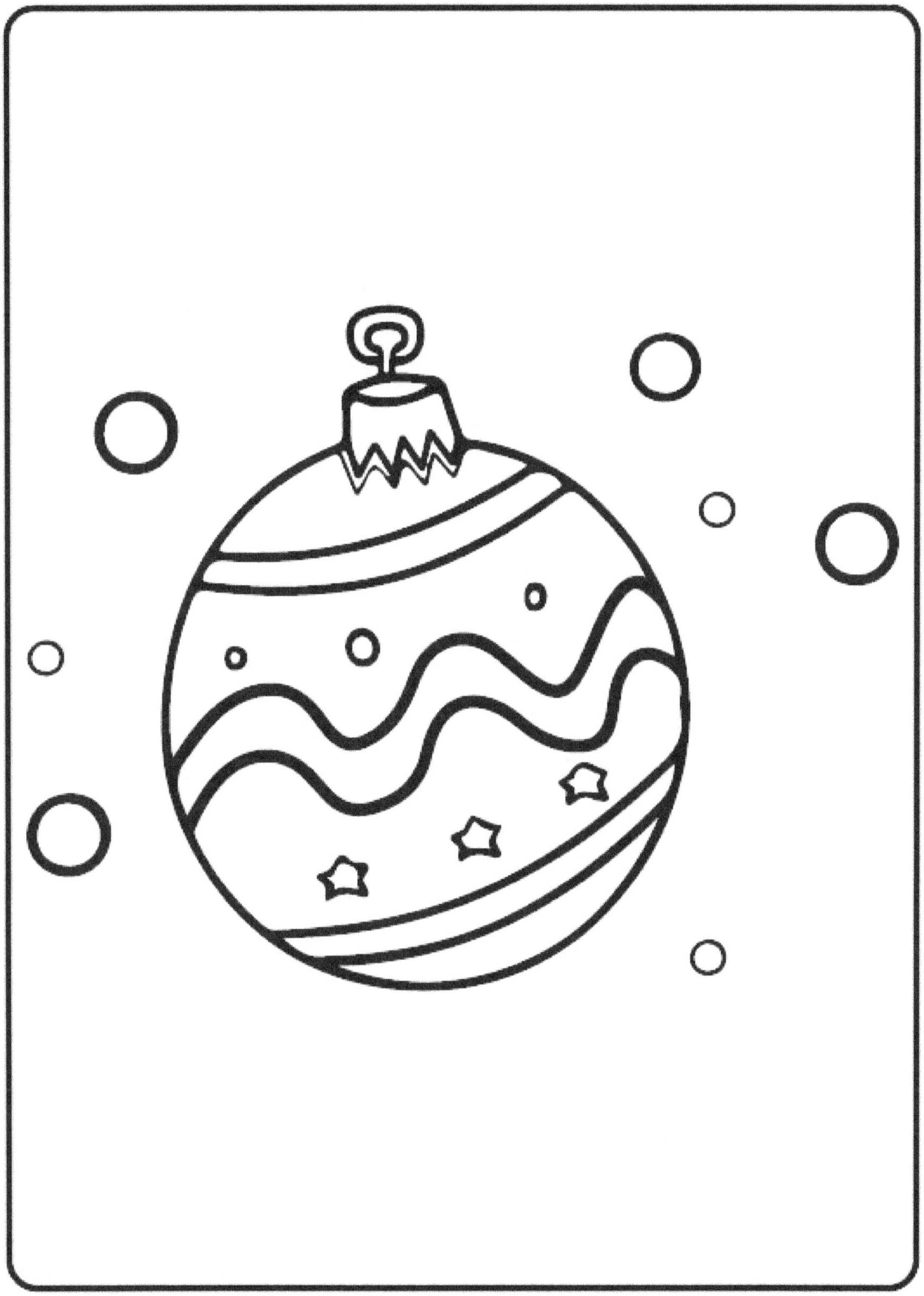

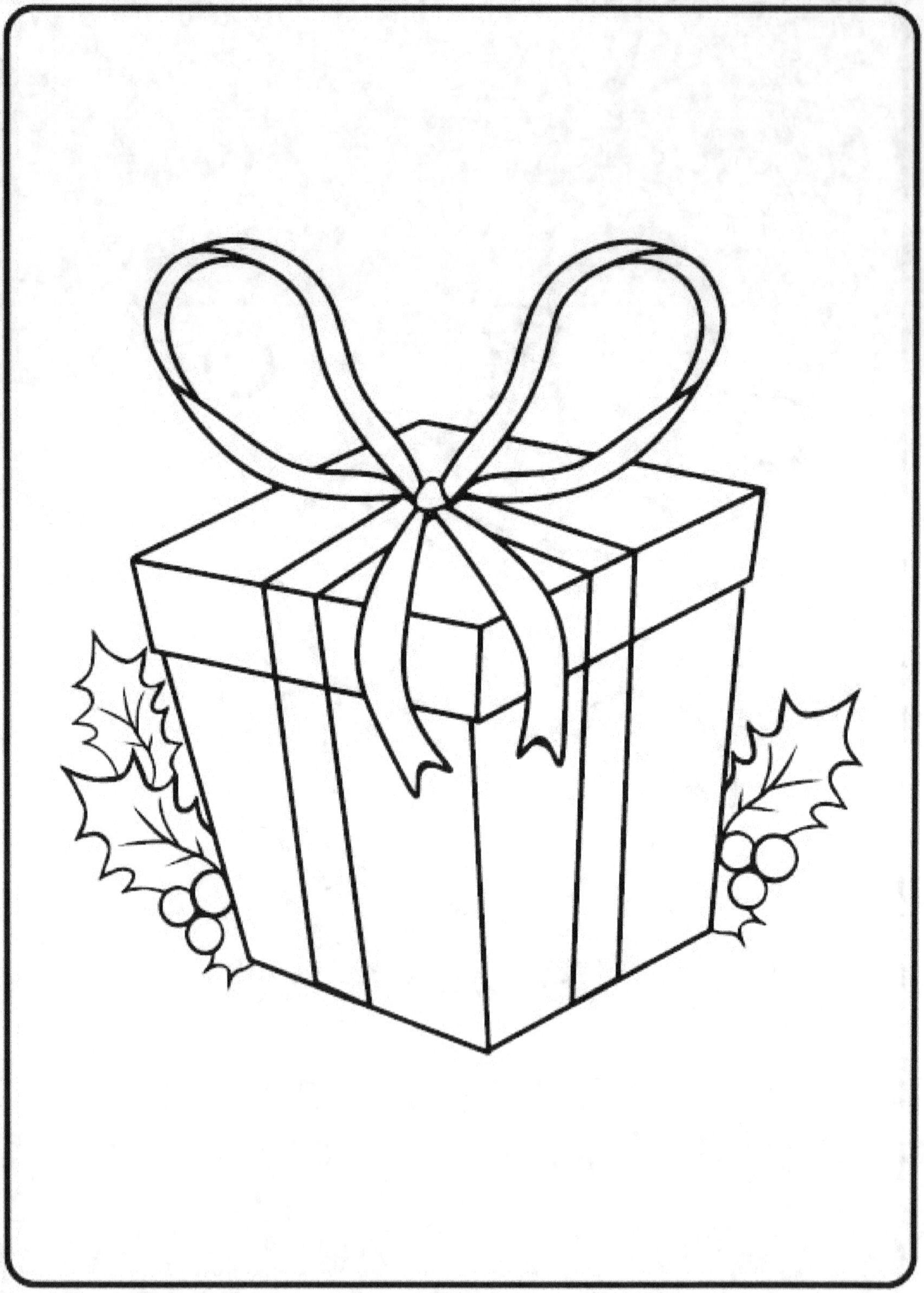

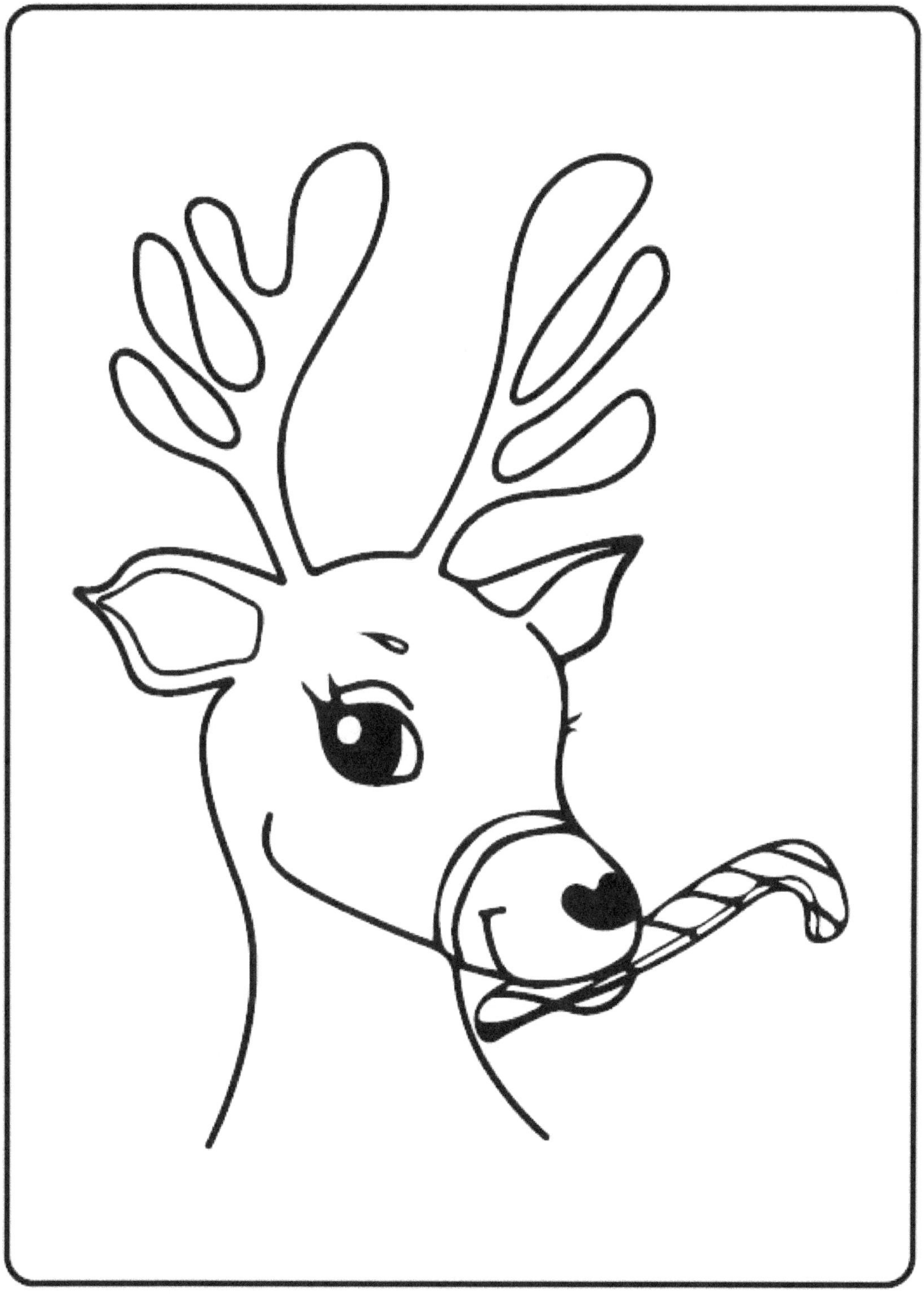

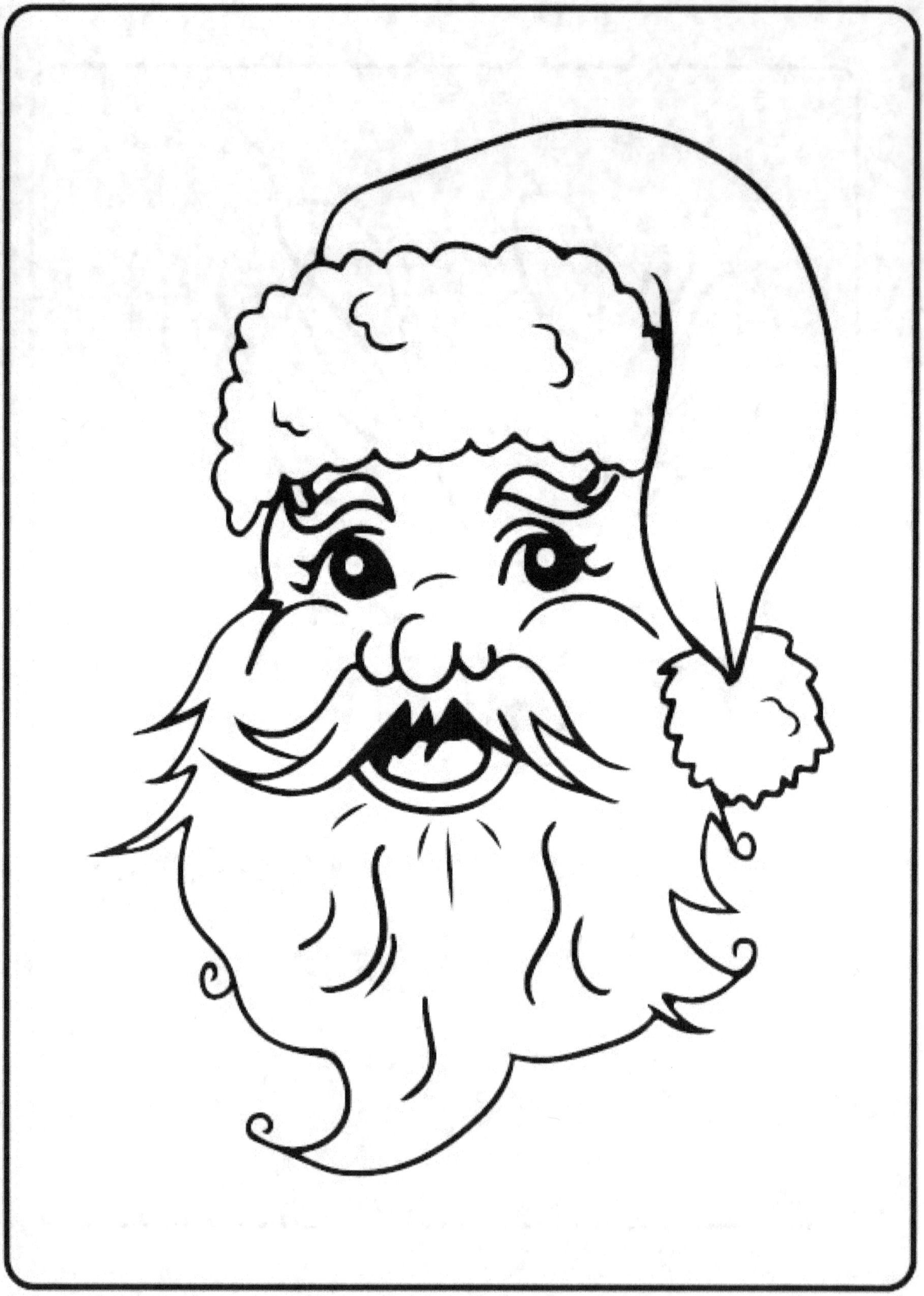

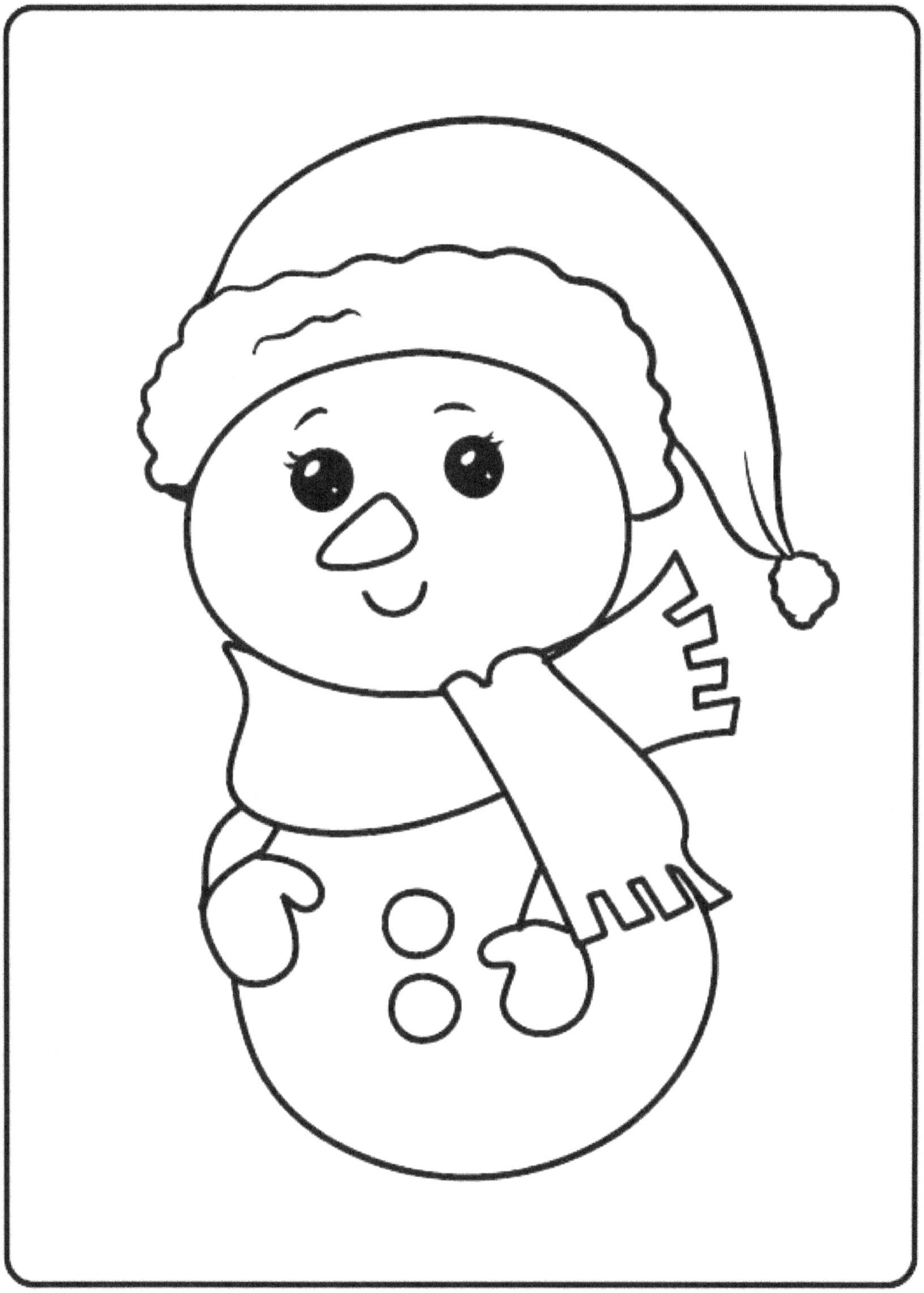

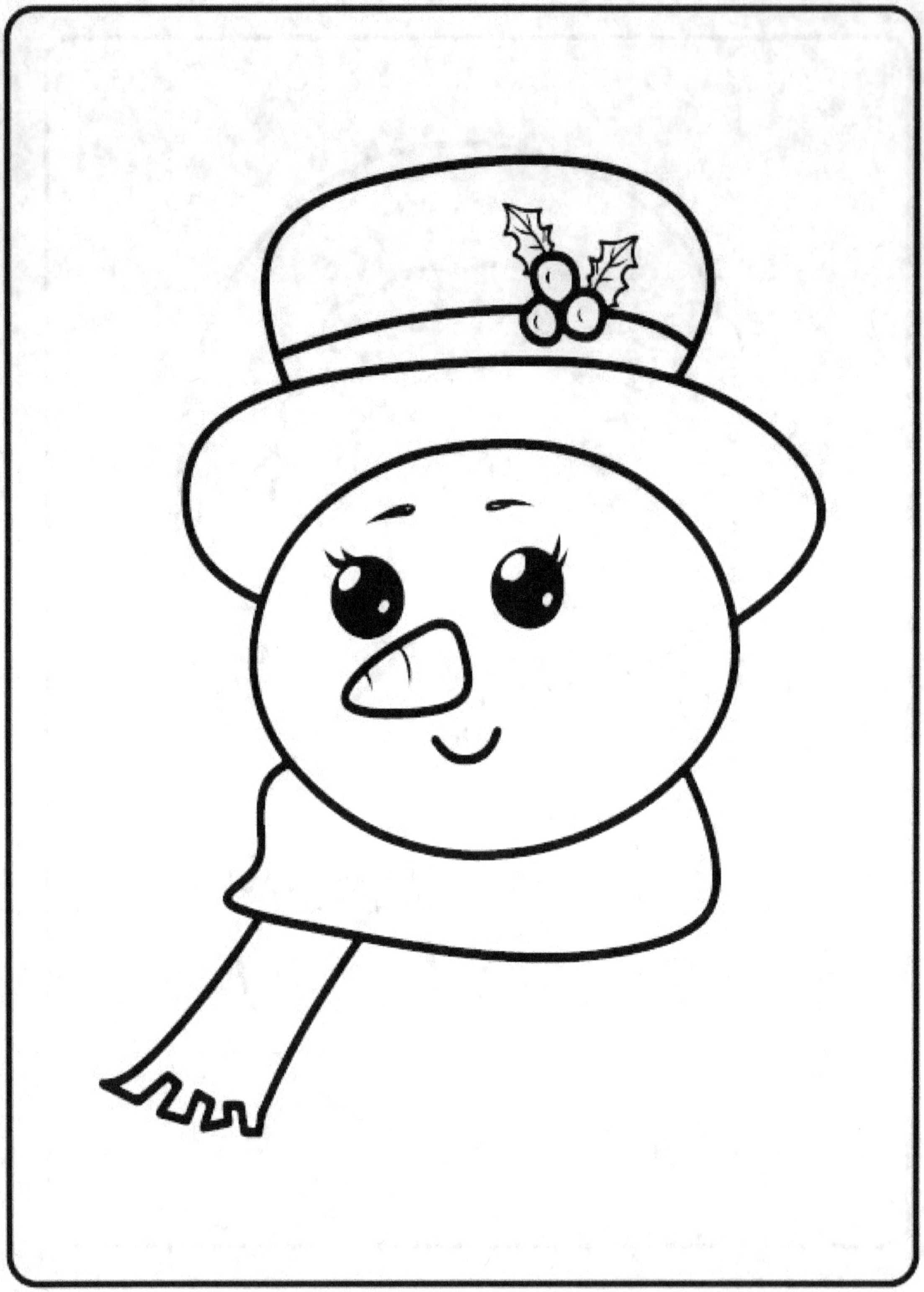

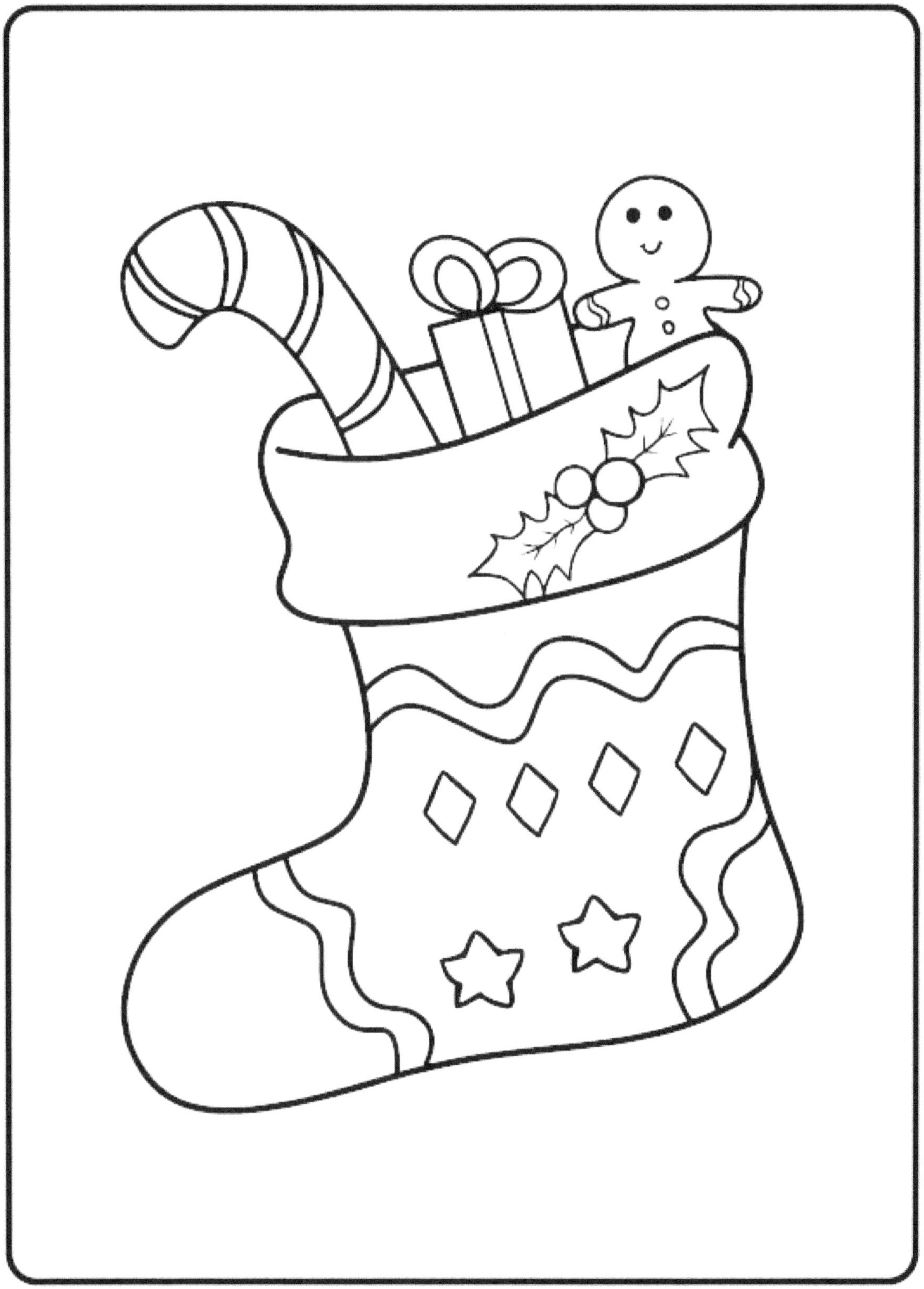

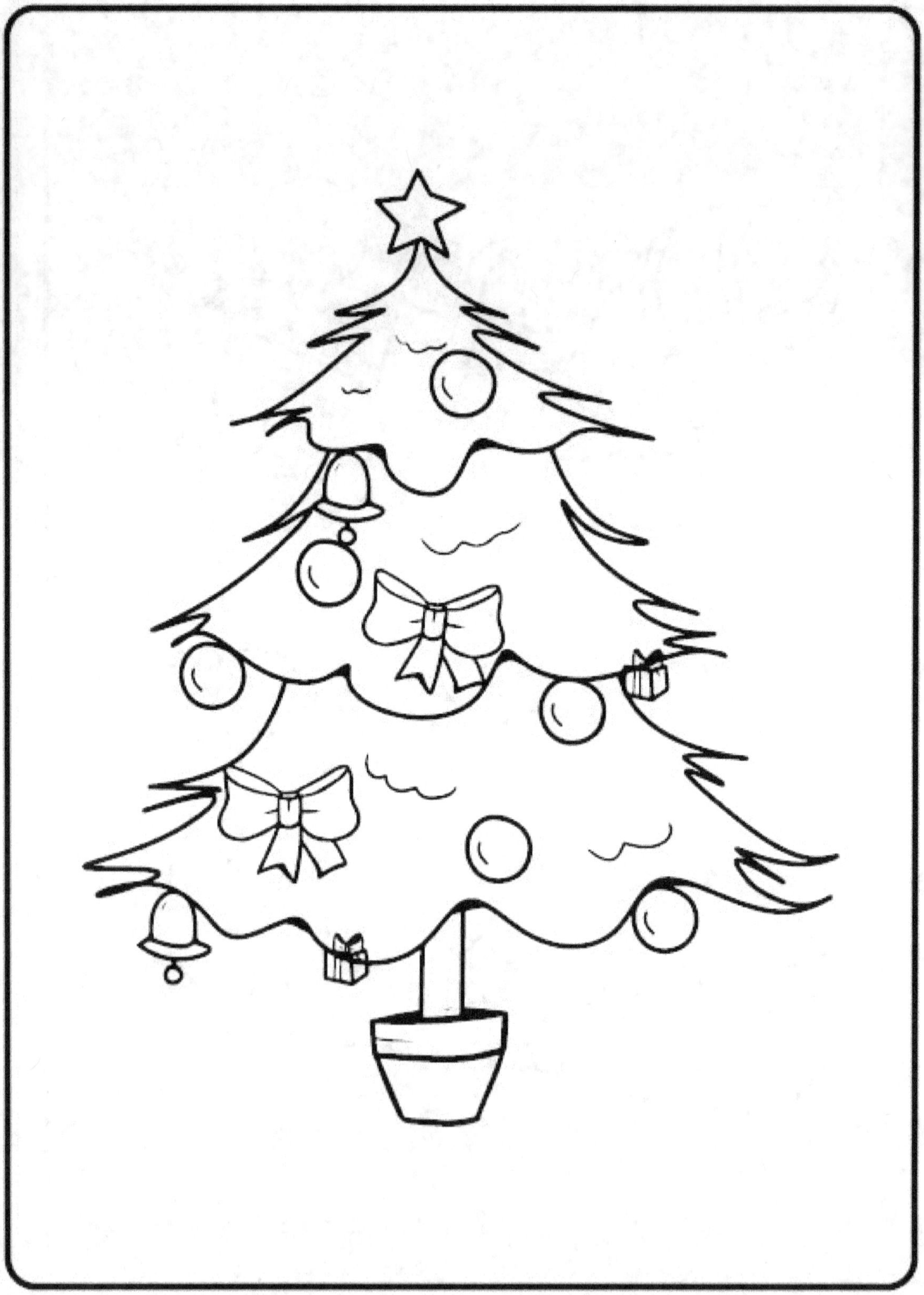

www.ingramcontent.com/pod-product-compliance
Lightning Source LLC
Chambersburg PA
CBHW082020230526
45466CB00022B/2920